BEI GRIN MACHT SICH IHR
WISSEN BEZAHLT

Bibliografische Information der Deutschen Nationalbibliothek:

Die Deutsche Bibliothek verzeichnet diese Publikation in der Deutschen National-
bibliografie; detaillierte bibliografische Daten sind im Internet über http://dnb.d-
nb.de/ abrufbar.

Impressum:

Copyright © 2015 GRIN Verlag
Druck und Bindung: Books on Demand GmbH, Norderstedt Germany
ISBN: 9783668673786

Dieses Buch bei GRIN:

https://www.grin.com/document/418384

Thomas Ohse

Teaching English as a Foreign Language in India

GRIN Verlag

GRIN - Your knowledge has value

Der GRIN Verlag publiziert seit 1998 wissenschaftliche Arbeiten von Studenten, Hochschullehrern und anderen Akademikern als eBook und gedrucktes Buch. Die Verlagswebsite www.grin.com ist die ideale Plattform zur Veröffentlichung von Hausarbeiten, Abschlussarbeiten, wissenschaftlichen Aufsätzen, Dissertationen und Fachbüchern.

Besuchen Sie uns im Internet:

http://www.grin.com/

http://www.facebook.com/grincom

http://www.twitter.com/grin_com

Start-Termin: Montag, 30. Dezember 2014

Abgabe-Termin: Montag, 02.März 2015

Teaching English as a Foreign Language in India

A Bachelor – Thesis

by
Thomas Ohse, MA

Contents

I The Role of English in India   **1**

  1   The British Period (1800 – 1947)   1

  2   Independence   3

  3   Is English a Foreign Language in India ?   5

  4   The Global Use of English   6

II Evolution of Teaching Methods in India   **8**

  1   The Vedic Period (ca. 4000–1000 BCE)   8

  2   The Brahmanic / Later Vedic Period (1000–500 BC)   9

  3   The Jainistic Period (since ca. 100 BCE)   9

  4   Buddhistic Education (500 BCE – 200 AD)   10

  5   The Muslim Period (1200 – 1858)   12

  6   Gandi's Education Philosophy   13

  7   Independence, since 1947   17

III Today   **20**

  1   The Ministry of Human Resource and Development   20

  2   The Department of School Education and Literacy   21

  3   The National Council for Teacher Education   21

  4   The Indian School System   22

  5   General Education   22

  6   Higher Secondary Education   23

  7   English as a Medium in School   23

Bibliography   **24**

List of Figures   **25**

List of Abbreviations   **25**

  Appendix   **27**

Abstract

India is often called a museum of teaching methods. That is because, in India still the direct method and other structural approaches are used. From the German point of view these methods are interesting, because in German teacher education, these methods are banned and therefore cannot be used or studied. It is the more interesting for a teacher in practical work to have knowledge about these relatively old methods of teaching, because they have their positive sides.

It is one big goal of this work to have a look at the positive sides of structural approaches in English language teaching.

These might be observed in India.

First of all, we want to have a look at the role of English in India

I The Role of English in India

1 The British Period (1800 – 1947)

When the British came to India, the school system was a large network of schools all over the country. Most of the villages had their own primary school, with a single teacher teaching one multiple class, where senior students acted as monitors to help the teacher. The teachers were badly trained and paid even less salaries.

In the beginning of the British occupation, mostly Christian missionaries built institutions where education was provided and they used education also as a means of Christianization.

By the end of the eighteenth century, when the East India Company (EIC) had brought all India under its control, its leaders started thinking about the education of the inhabitants. Before that, there had only been education for British people, organized by the EIC. To educate the natives was a strategy whose ulterior aim was to create a feeling of awe and respect for Europeans among Indians. Between 1824 and 1835, classes in English were started and the first British schools were established. Among the Indians, there was a certain demand for Western knowledge. English was the language of education, it was the medium of instruction and it was also used for the dissemination of Western morals and values. There was a possibility of English becoming the language of the Far East so English would become the language of commerce.

In 1834, Lord Macaulay had been made chief of the Public Instruction. He decided that only a selected few could be educated. He wanted to educate "[..] a class of persons Indian in blood and colour, but English in tastes, in opinions, in morals and in intellect." Macaulay (1835) Through filtration, education would then percolate to the masses. During Macaulay's regency there was a rapid growth of English schools and colleges in India. The education was characterized by English ideals, religious neutrality and English was the medium of instruction. In the words of (Krishnaswamy and Krishnaswamy 2006: 39), Macaulay "transplanted" the "alien system" Krishnaswamy and Krishnaswamy (2006: 42) from Britain to India.

In 1853 when the Charter Act, the law defining the role of the EIC, came up for renewal, Indians were allowed for Civil Services Examination but English remained the language of administration. This raised the for English in India a lot.

In 1857, three universities were started in Chennai, Mumbai and Colcatta. In 1858 the Crown took over form the EIC. India was a British colony.

Around the end of the 19th century, a university degree had become a passport for a to sure employment in the administration. The passport to the university was the school-leaving certificate. As a result. English medium schools sprang up in and around the university towns. English had become a "prestige language" (Krishnaswamy and Krishnaswamy 2006: 54) in India. It was the language of education, commerce, and administration. A job in Government service was a mark of status in India among the educated class. English education was producing "gentlemen-clerks of the most obedient type" (Krishnaswamy and Krishnaswamy 2006: 79).

The concept of a printed book did not exist until the sixteenth century, when the Europeans brought the printing press to India. Since the printers had problems printing the vernacular languages, it was an advantage for the English language. 130 newspapers and periodicals were established around 1838 to 1851. Printing had also not been involved in education, learning was mostly imparted through the oral mode, books were rare. The expansion of the print-media also expanded the growth of English in urban areas.

The introduction of railway lines and telegraph and postal services encouraged communication in English. The widening urban network with the new communication facilities helped English, Western technology and trade. All of this was rising the demand for competence in English.

The common language assisted the growth of unity of thought among the educated class of India. English was beginning to become the lingua franca of India. Many graduates, who received their degrees in Mumbai, Colcata, Chennai and other cities, went to Britain to complete their education at one of the British universities.

In 1902, the Indian universities Commission stated that "many students pass through the entire university without [...] command of the language." (cited after Krishnaswamy and Krishnaswamy 2006: 65).

In 1904, Lord Curzon (Fig. 2) drew the attention of the government to education policy: "Ever since the cold breath of Macaulay's rhetoric passed over the field of Indian languages and Indian Textbooks the elementary education of the people in their own language has shrivelled and pined." (Pattanayak 1990: 17) Lord Curzon thought that the Indian model represented a "slavish imitation" (Krishnaswamy and Krishnaswamy 2006: 65) of the English model and stated that Indian education was a "mere shell without a kernel in it" (Krishnaswamy and Krishnaswamy 2006: 65). As a result, the study of vernacular was allowed incipiently at the lower levels after 1902. After three or four years of schooling in the mother tongue, English was taught. These streams were available in addition to the English-medium schools. The Government felt that students who had been through a complete vernacular stream, were mentally more efficient. But English continued to be the language of higher education. Curzon established teacher training institutions at various levels. He raised the standard of higher education by re-organization, he reformed the curriculum and introduced grant in aid, mother tongue as a medium of instruction became common at the primary stage of education and founded scholarships for studying aboard.

In the 1920s, the English-educated class took over the English language and started changing its character. The nationalist movement stripped made the language a tool of communication for projecting national aspirations and sensibilities. As a result, even the Declaration of Independence by Pandit Jawaharlal Nehru on 15th August 1947 was written in English language.

2 Independence

On July 1st 1947, the British Parliament passed the the Indian Independence Act. India became a Republic on January 26th 1950. The Indian constitution was written in English. Jawaharlal Nehru, the first Prime Minister of India, stated that, on the long run, Hindi should become the national language, but for an indefinite period, people of "non-Hindi areas" (Krishnaswamy and Krishnaswamy 2006: 113) should be able to correspond with their government in English.

The administration and the judiciary continued to use English. The railway, post and telecommunication network and bureaucracy was also still transacting in English.

But the English language became disliked by the nationalistic movement. But the will of nationalists to throw out then English language together with the British met the resistance of those, who had come to power by English education and they had the support of others who were saying, that the English language was the unifying power in India which also helped organizing the resistance against the British occupation.

When in 1960, President Rajendra Prasad tried to make Hindi the language of the Supreme Court and all High Courts, there were immediate repercussions in the non-Hindi areas. There even were riots by an anti-Hindi movement in the south in 1965. The government remembered Nehru's assurance and decided that every state should have complete freedom to transact its business in the language of its own choice, communication from one state to another should be either in English or accompanied by an English translation, and English would be used as the language of transaction at the central level. In 1967 an law was passed which said: "English will continue as an associate official language for an indefinite period." (Krishnaswamy and Krishnaswamy 2006: 123).

Since Hindi was not accepted by the other regions, English continued to be the academic language, because it was necessary for the academic staff, to publish and communicate with other Indian regions.

The first English Language Teaching Institute (ELTI) had been established in Allahabad in 1954 with the collaboration of the British Council. The structural approach (audio-lingual method, oral-aural method, situational method) was accepted in India and replaced the grammar-translation method. In 1958 the Central Institute of English and Foreign Languages was established in Hyderabad in collaboration with the British Council. Its objective was to train teachers of English, produce English teaching materials and help to improve the standard of English teaching in India. A Regional Institute of English for South India (RIE) was established in Bangalore in 1963. A second RIE was set up in Chandigarh and more than twelve ELTIs all over India, conducting teacher training and producing materials. Some states started State Institutes of English, others

4

appointed special officers for English teaching, attached to the Directorates of Education. District centres were also started for the training of teachers at the school level in some states.

Teaching English Literature (TELI) was a humanistic discipline which was supposed to have ennobling and mind-training properties. The standard canon of English literature was Chaucer, Shakespeare, Milton, Dryden, Pope, Wordsworth, Coleridge, Shelley and Browning. No serious attempt was made to evolve indigenous approaches to the teaching of English in India. There was no attempt to redefine teaching English in post-colonial India. As Krishnaswamy and Krishnaswamy (2006: 137)put it:

> "'Teaching was (and is even now) carried on mechanically as a ritual without any involvement whatsoever on the part of teachers or learners; the whole exercise was (and is) examination-degree-centred and market-driven.'"

But"English in India has become international oriented than British oriented. "(Krishnaswamy and Krishnaswamy 2006: 140)

By the turn of the 20th century, there were more users of English in India than in Britain. There is a huge range of dialects, accents and varieties and English is also the state language Nagaland and Meghalaya.

3   Is English a Foreign Language in India ?

In the terminology of Crystal (2012) English in India is a second language (L$_2$). In the three-circle model of Kachru (2006) it is located in the "'outer circle'" of English. English as a foreign language is the circle where English is taught and learned as a foreign language (FL). English is not considered as a foreign language in India but it's also not included in the list of officially recognized languages of India. (Krishnaswamy and Krishnaswamy 2006: 145) state that "the status of English in India is unique.".

> "English of Indians is neither a foreign language nor a second language nor a dialect of English – it is a *modulect*, a 'lect' that works as a module."
> (Krishnaswamy and Krishnaswamy 2006: 169)

"'The wide spread use of English in India and the large number of Indians using it, has resulted in a distinct variety, that maybe called 'Indian English'.'" (Krishnaswamy and Krishnaswamy 2006: 143)

Indian English is English as a second language. There is no baby talk in English to make it a home language. For the majority of the English-educated people, English is a street or office language. English in India is domain-specific and register-based: for bureaucratic, administrative, academic, legal, technical and scientific purposes, for creative writing, journalism and other limited social purposes.

The Oxford English dictionary lists about 1000 words of Indian origin. More than 1000 words of English origin are used in every Indian language. Even in rural areas, words like motor, car, switch, bus, train, stamp, letter etc were used in India from the beginning. Still today, the rural areas are affected by English words and culture from television.

English is not really a foreign language to India. India was occupied for 150 years. The English established the Indian school system. And still, English is a tool of communication in many parts of Indian life. "'Teaching English as Forgeign Language"' means to start from scartch. Like there was no English in the life of the student whatsoever. This is of course not the case. There are English television shows, English signs everywhere, there is English plates on the shops and government and train company buildings. When indians grow up, English has a lot of influence in their life. But the English teacher cannot make a difference, if someone already knows some English words or English chunks. Of course it's a good starting point. But the main things, like grammar, literature, the rules of writing (orthography) all the basics, they have to learn like it was a foreign language, English is not the mother tongue and it is not even close to bilingual use. The better term would be teaching English as a second language.

4   The Global Use of English

English has become part of the IT revolution. It is spoken by 1.5 billion people around the world. 350 million people use English as a mother tongue; the rest as a foreign or second language. English language no longer a language of national, cultural or class identity. English is the language of the Internet. 80% of the websites use English and 3/4 of all the world's mail, telexes and cables are in English. Most of the software is in English and all the IT giants, like Microsoft, Macintosh and IBM are based in English speaking countries. English is the language that contains all the knowledge in all the disciplines. Even China has adopted a policy to make every student literate in English and Singapore has declared English as its common language. As a result, the English is changing. It is losing its culture, class and race. It has become a tool for international communication. Since English has become international, it does not belong to any one culture. This cultural neutrality has made it acceptable for a vast majority of people all over the world. English for professional purposes like facing interviews, writing resumes, writing reports, conducting campaigns, writing letters, participating in meetings, seminars, conferences, and discussions, are demanded. That is the ability to communicate one's ideas and attitudes is the expected skill and not the ability to interpret a literary text. It is communication skills in English that have a worldwide market, because English has become the language of business and commerce, trade, technology, journalism, electronic media, the Internet and IT-services. If one's accent is internationally intelligible, the market is wide open for an Indian.

The increasing employment opportunities for English-knowing educated Indians have made the English language acceptable for a vast majority of people of contemporary India . English is a global advantage for India over countries like China. "'India is at peace with English"'(Krishnaswamy and Krishnaswamy 2006: 157). Even states ruled by communist parties have changed their English language policies, because English is no longer viewed as a class barrier. "English for all" (Krishnaswamy and Krishnaswamy 2006: 157) is the new slogan. Indians have realized that English is no longer a symbol of colonialism but a tool for international communication. Since English is used all over the world, people in different countries have made it a medium to express their own cultures.

With the advent of the IT revolution, the demand for English has increased. There is a big motivation to become computer and English-literate. Lots or jobs were created for Indians during the era of globalization in outsourcing centres, call, centres, medical transcriptions centres, book-keeping for various multinational companies, software development etc. India is providing cheap and skilled labour for multinational companies. Highly qualified Indians are teaching English in many parts of the world. Many foreigners come to India for medical treatment, to learn yoga or even for employment. All this is only possible because India speaks English.

This move away from from an elitist use of English might change the demographics of the English speaking population in India. Then English will become a second language for most Indians in all registers without restrictions.

II The Structural Approach

Haß (2012) s. 16/17 Neuner (2003: 229) Pattern Drill Neuner(2003): Vermittlungsmethoden: Historischer Überblick. In: Bausch Krumm: Handbuch Fremdsprachenunterricht 225-235 BFS 5047 Zimmermann (1997: 10): "intensive oral drilling of sentence patterns" BFS7895 Savinion (2001: 17) Modell der kommunikativen Komperen In: Teaching English as a Foreign Language. Marianne Celce-Murcua. 13-28 ENE 2121

III Original Teaching Methods in India

Education in India has a long Tradition.

From the stand-point of an educational philosopher, the period of ancient India is the most interesting. During this period there were four different schools of thought/religion active in India: the Vedic, the Brahmanic, the Jainistic and the Buddhistic.

Since this work is primarily concerned with today's issues, there will only have a brief overview, to understand today's culture of education in India.

1 The Vedic Period (ca. 4000–1000 BCE)

During the Vedic Period knowledge was considered the third eye of man which gives him insight into all worldly and non-worldly matters. During this period, students stayed with their Teacher (Guru) in his or her house for up to 12 years and became a part of the family. Teaching was considered a holy duty which a Brahama (an educated person) was bound to discharge for free. Place of education was generally the forest.

The methods of instruction consisted generally of recitation by the teacher and repetition by the pupil. There was a strong emphasis on correct pronunciation, intonation and articulation. Since there were no books, knowledge depended on correct repetition. Meditation was another step in Vedic education which was followed by a discussion between the teacher and the student. Students were taught individually not by class method. The teaching followed some strategies: simple to complex, activity to skill-oriented procedures, Question-Answer technique and illustration (drastanta). However, self-study (swaadhyaya) was considered most important. The oral character preserved in Indian education until today. Self-control and self-discipline was considered the best discipline but corporal punishment was not altogether ruled out.

Education was not all about knowledge. Main features of Vedic education were the emphasis on freedom from material desires. It was also moral, religious and spiritual. The very environment in which students lived was calculated to give a proper turn to their character. Students were directly under the supervision of the teacher who was to watch not only their academic attainment. In everyday life, students were made to follow the rules of etiquette and good manners towards their seniors, equals, and juniors. The rules helped in the formation of what was seen as a good character. Rituals and daily prayers also helped to form moral habits. Even today there is the morning prayer in every Indian school [1]. It mainly has an organizing character but also involves praying and/or mediation.

Demerits of the Vedic education were that there was a very rigid way of instruction and an the emphasis on strict discipline. It did not encourage any self-expression of the pupils but complete surrender to the rules of the Vedas. Also a demerit of Instruction was that it primarily depended on verbal instructions. It required repetition and encouraged rote learning, which also still is a big part of Indian education[2] Also, there was no separation of knowledge and religion. Hinduistic values like tolerance, non-violence, freedom, equality, justice, brotherhood and harmony were very important topics in Vedic education. Vedic education was learner-centred, attention was paid to the students interests, aptitude, proficiency and performance.

2 The Brahmanic / Later Vedic Period (1000–500 BC)

This period has different names in literature. Singh (2011) calls it Brahmanic Period, Aggarwal (2004), in accordance with Wikipedia[3], calls it Later Vedic Period. We can observe a shift from oral to literal education. Also, Education became denied to women and Shudras (4th Caste). Brahmanic education was dominated by religion. Education was viewed as a preparation for life here and after (death). Due to absence of collective education, Brahmanic education centred on the individual, its growth and development but curriculum became more universal than in Vedic education. Practical education had a special place in the programme. Education was marked by rituals and the teaching methodology was centred around listening, contemplation, comprehension, self-study and recall.

---

[1] A good example can be found at https://www.youtube.com/watch?v=6t-wyr-Ahl0
[2] Compare: https://www.youtube.com/watch?v=qsQZUKCn_l8
[3] http://en.wikipedia.org/wiki/Vedic_period

3   The Jainistic Period (since ca. 100 BCE)

In Jainism, there are ive vows (*vrata*): not to injure, not to utter falsehood, not to steal, to lead a celibate life and to to renounce the world, which practically means chastity and contentment. The vow of non-violence (*Ahimsa*) was seen very strictly, in word, thought and action. Individualistic aspects were emphasized. The aim of life was seen as to get oneself disentangled from karma[4]. The ultimate goal of Jainism is *Moksha* i.e., the dissolution of partnership between soul and matter.

Truth was seen as relativistic and pluralistic. This means, knowledge is not fixed. Education focused on divinity and the elimination of the material bond of the soul. Education had to lead to self-enlightenment and restoration of the powers of the soul (*jiva*). There was an emphasis on the development of the individual personality. Knowledge (*jnana*) and penance were seen as vehicles to help the soul to disentangle from Karma. Cessation of Karma was the meaning of life. Due to the believe of the transmigration of the soul (*jiva*), education partly also already prepares for the next world. Education should develop a sense of discrimination between merit (*punya*) and sin (*paap*). Therefore, it should include provision for attainment of the three vows (faith, knowledge and conduct), the principles of life that bring happiness, success and love. Also, Education should include non-violence as a virtue, practised and not only aspired for. Knowledge is thought, senses and meditation. Therefore, teaching had to develop these faculties. Teaching should be social and tolerant and should bring happiness to all. The soul (*Jiva*) is essentially karmic (related to action), therefore, education must be action-based and ideally oriented. Therefore, Jainistic education put great emphasis on self-discipline and hard work. Practical discipline was essential for the release of the soul from the bondage of sin and desires. Happiness and bliss were achieved through action. Man is a free moral agent, responsible for all his deliberate action.

During Vedic Education, Education was conduced in the Gurukul or teacher's house. Students lived as members of the family. The emphasis was on the study of the Veda. Sanskrit was the medium of education. Brahmans were the teachers. Education was not available to every class of society. Education was free. The students' life was rigorous. Sanskrit was taught. No common schools. Teacher was supreme and students devoid of freedom. No provision of co-education.

---

[4]   Karma means action, causality or effect. A soul tainted with karma is viewed as a soul in bondage

4 Buddhistic Education (500 BCE – 200 AD)

Buddhistic education was characterized by a broad and comprehensive, positivistic and practical attitude which aimed at liberation, a cordial relationship between teacher and taught, a homely educational climate with emphasis on character formation and development of an ideal value system.

Buddhistic education came into existence in the 5th century B.C., in India. Brahman education deprived the common people of their right to education. The Buddhist education system was based on the system of the Vedic period but took it place in assemblies (*Sanghas*). Demerits are that there was too much focus made on scriptures. This made education narrow and conservative, and failed to develop a capacity of independent thinking and reasoned recourse. It was in this period that the method of collective teaching and the presence of numerous teachers in a single institution was invented. Social instead of individual methods of teaching. Education was institutionalized. There was provision of co-education in Buddhist education. In Buddhist Education, Education was imparted in schools or universities.

Every class of society, except the Chandals (disposers of the dead) had the right to receive education. Education was for all in equal measure regardless of caste and creed. Education began at the age of eight. After attaining the age of 20, students were qualified to become monks. The determination of a minimum age for higher education, the providing of a set of rules and the taking of a test for admission were invented during this period.

Students were ordinated to obey ten rules which included (Singh 2011: 37): abstaining from theft, killing of any living being, use of intoxicating things, use of cosmetics, watching dances or listening to music, etc. Students were required to serve their teachers, eat food thrice a day, wear three items of clothes, bathe themselves with pure water and live in discipline. Initially women were prohibited from joining a *Sangha* (monastery) but later on they were granted admission. A fee was payable in some form or the other.

The syllabus during this period was comprehensive. Education was universal. Language of teaching was vernacular language to address all social levels. The education syllabus was divided into religious and material. In Buddhistic education, knowledge has no metaphysical value for life. It only has value if it works and brings desired results. Singh speaks of a positivistic approach: "Truth is knowledge in action." (Singh 2011: 40). Whatever works is true and good. Education must prepare the child to understand and deal with changing situations. Therefore, a varied and comprehensive curriculum with special reference to philosophy, logic, grammar and ethics was taught to enable students to acquire a rational, critical and righteous way of life.

Three stages of the educative process helped to develop a habit of knowledge assimilation: pondering and reflection, self-study and national attitude.

Buddhism disappeared from India as a result of the "Brahmanic renaissance"(Mann 1995: 61) Non-violence weakened the country militarily.

5   The Muslim Period (1200 – 1858)

A synthesis between materialistic and religious education began and consequently, a tendency towards professionalization and vocationalization. Eduction had achieved objectivity. Education already became compulsory, but only for Muslim children and teachers lost their high status in society. Prime objectives of Muslim education were: propagation of religion, worldly progress and strengthening of the administration.

Around 1200 BC, India was beginning to become occupied by Persia the Persians learned all the scientific elements in philosophy, mathematics, astronomy, medicine and chemistry from India during the 8th and 9th century (Krishnaswamy and Krishnaswamy 2006: 4). Persian became state language. The Hindus learned it to get government jobs. The Muslim rulers helped to develop the art of history writing.

During the Muslim Period, there was a strong emphasis on reading, mostly the Koran. Islam recommends knowledge and education. The Koran ordains man to read and teach. Education is sacred as it was Allah who educated the first man. Prophet Mohammad declared (Singh 2011: 48): "To seek knowledge is a religious duty for every Muslim, man and woman."

Muslim education reached its zenith during the Moghul period (1526 – 1858). But there was no systematic and consistent educational policy under the Muslim Kings. During the Muslim period, education developed very slow. Nevertheless, according to Singh (2011), Muslim education left an indelible mark on Indian life.

Education began in the Maktab, i.e., a primary school. First, there was the *Bismillah*, a ritual , which was performed at the age of 4 years, 4 month and 4 days. Still today, parents send there children to school at this age, although, the government doesn't want them to. The *Maulvis* (teachers) taught the alphabet along with verses from the Koran. Generally, most Maktabs were appendages of mosques. Higher education was provided by the Madrassas which sometimes had hostels integrated. Education was imparted by lectures. Knowledge was given to students directly and individually by experts through a system of apprenticeship. The most prevalent method was the oral method. Individual attention was paid to students. Teachers received a low salary, but they had an important place in society and commanded respect and trust. It was believed that the students who served their teachers made God happy. To maintain order and discipline, there was a system of severe punishment, but brilliant scholars were also rewarded. After receiving education, the child should be capable of earning his/her livelihood. The spread of education only from practical and materialistic viewpoint led to education in manual skills, sculpture, agriculture, medicine, military science, painting,housing construction, manufacture of weapons, etc. In the educational system, the emphasis was not on integral development; it was on reading and writing. Self-study was no longer important and was therefore not encouraged.

The schools were owned privately or by the state. There was encouragement by the state for education. Irrespective of their religion and faith, the educated people were offed posts of Kazis (dispenser of justice) and Wazirs (ministers). Some rulers provided aid to Maktabs and Madrassas, for satisfaction of their interests. Also, the rulers need educated people for the writing of the histories of their period of reigns. The political instability made the Madrassas and Maktabs short-lived because they depended on the good-will of the ruler and his donations.

Only the affluent received education, education was limited to towns and education of women was completely neglected.

6   Gandi's Education Philosophy

Under the chairmanship of Gandhi, the following principles were formulated at Wardha: From the age of 7 – 14, education should be <u>free</u>, <u>compulsory</u> and <u>universal</u>[5]. Education should develop human values in the child. It should develop all the powers of the child according its community. Education should achieve the harmonious development of body, mind, heart and soul. It should employ some craft as medium of edu-

---

[5]   This phrase became a part of India's constitution later.

cation so that the pupil gains economic self-reliance. Education of all subjects should be imparted in the context of local crafts. Through productive work it should be self-supporting, lead to economic independence and self-reliance. All education should be impaired through correlation with an industry. This industry should be such that the student can gain work experience through practised work. Education should gain new experiences and bring forth new researches by engaging in various experiments. Education should create useful, responsible and dynamic citizens.

Mann (1995) summarizes the following characteristics of the English education system in India: the English education system was set up for the creation of an elite class. The British created a new caste or class: the British-educated, who lived in a world of their own. The education system was built up in the style of the liberal education concept of the middle class in nineteenth century England in which formal education was the entrance-ticket to a "'white-collar-profession'" (Mann 1995: 63).

The contempt for manual work, stemming from Brahmanic tradition, was increased by the English education system and transferred to other levels and castes. Education was authoritative an uncritical, with imitation and functional learning as its basic principles, without critical reflection. The uncritical acquisition of knowledge turned education into a reproductive process. Education was imparted to prepare pupils for service, not for life. Schools were "spirit deadening cramming machines" (Mann 1995: 64). The whole education system was oriented around the standard of the West. Education was a status symbol of an elite who disliked manual work.

According to Singh (2011: 127), Gandhi is the starting point of modern educational theory in the East. His Concept of *Basic Education* is also called a silent social revolution in the field of Indian education. Gandhi's philosophy is a dynamic concept. He went back to the roots of Hindusim and paid greater attention to the education of the personality. Gandhi's concept of education provides for the biological, sociological and psychological fulfilment of men's needs. He believed that education should bring about the development of the whole man. Education, in this sense, means to draw out the best from the child and the man: physically (body), intellectually (mind) and spiritually (spirit). Gandhi intended at the balanced development of the child to enable it to achieve the ultimate aim i.e. truth. He regards education and (economic) development as being closely interlinked. His goals and methods of education built on a system of normative propositions referring to a superior metaphysical norm of meaning. As a representative of normative education theory, Gandhi creates absolute standards of meaning about (wo)man's vocation and his (her) task in the world. In Hinduism, the fundamental goal of life is self-realization. Gandhi's theories centre on this goal. He exceeds the aspirations of Hinduism though, in his demand for simultaneous spiritualization and practical realization of social end ethical values. For Gandhi, truth is synonymous with God and the opposite of truth is selfishness. Non-Violence (*A-Himsa*) is a godly ideal, man has to strive for. The selfless human, who finds self-fulfilment in selfless conduct, could be seen as the goal of Gandhi's teaching. The way of non-violence is achieved by love. Love leads to the recognition of truth. Man must recognize and children must learn that love will triumph over hate, truth over falsehood and humility over violence. *A-himsa* is a "'categorical imperative"'(Mann 1995: 63), in which selfishness and ambitions (*Himsa*), should be overcome. Mohandas Gandhi stands between 'Sanskitization' and 'Westernization'. On the one hand he endeavours to break up the most hardened structure of the caste system but on the other hand he warns of the consequences of Western influences. He is against Varnarism (Brahmanic conservatism esp. affirmation of the caste system) as well as he is against Colonialism. According to Krishnaswamy and Krishnaswamy (2006: 7)

> "Colonialism is the practise by which a powerful country controls less powerful countries and uses their resources in order to further its own interests, wealth and power."　　　　　　　　　　　　　　　　　　　　　　　—

Gandhi demanded a turning away from the existing Western education system because it was based on a foreign culture and excluded the indigenous culture, it ignored the culture of "the heart and the hand" and "confines itself to the head" (Mann 1995: 65).

His educational philosophy can be summarized as follows. The Child is the centre of education, the aim of education is the development of a child's personality. Children have to realize the dignity of labour and be respectful toward it. Therefore, education should centre on activity, it should be objective-centred and useful, it should provide an understanding of the unity of knowledge and it should help to instill the quality of morality and foster ideal citizenship. Basic crafts should help to make students self-supporting. Various (resp. all) subjects should be taught through craft. Teachers and students should be given maximum freedom for work. Mother-tongue should be the medium of instruction.

"I [...] regard it as a sin against the mother-land to inflict upon her children a tongue other than their mother's for their development" (Krishnaswamy and Krishnaswamy 2006: 89)

He also thought that real education was impossible through a foreign language. He thought it would put "a strain upon the pupil" to learn by heart and not on understanding (Mann 1995: 71). Finally, the restriction to functional learning should be rejected and the "'integral education and development'" (Mann) of the personality was called for.

It's worth mentioning though, that his suggestions are all in English language. Gandhi assumes, that man lives in a community. This establishes social and ethical values such as tolerance, mutual service and community spirit. We can regard this community education as one of Gandhi's "pedagogic keystones" (Mann 1995: 69). The community education should develop democratic behaviour.

When Gandhi calls for an integral education, i.e. starting from the unity of soul, body and spirit, a particularistic over-emphasis and over-rating of single areas (e.g. geometry, algebra, geography, literature) should be encountered. In the background stands the criticism of a curriculum which consists of exclusively cognitive teaching content, which abstracts from the concrete geographical social and economic environment of the pupil and neglects the development of manual and physical skills. The pupil should not be removed from his immediate field of experience, but should develop his knowledge and way of life with the members of his family and his village, and in integration with the environment. He was also pro co-education because in the families boys and girls grow up together as well.

The English rulers introduced a method of education which aimed at developing the individuality of the student but was not concerned about the use to which this individuality could be put. It was utilized not in the service of others but for exploiting them. Gandhi's *Basic Education* included the whole village in the process of education. Education had become more wide spread.

In the anglicized school system the lessons are oriented around the textbook and the syllabus, based upon the method of teaching through a passive listening of ideas.

In the context of *Basic Education* the school lesson is oriented around the immediate life situation of the pupil and the underlying syllabus, as worked out at the Wardha

Conference. The teaching should develop exclusively around the subject of experience. The securing of one's own nourishment, the desire for cleanliness, worry about one's health, and the conditions for a harmonic human co-existence in a community are all examples of reference points towards which the formal knowledge (mathematics, biology, etc.) is to be learnt.

Gandhi's philosophy is characterized by idealistic features. With the foundations truth, justice, non-violence, community and cooperation, the goal of education should be reached. Manual work, as a medium of instruction, stands in the middle of Gandhi's education concept. Since the whole spectrum of formal schooling is not covered by manual work, the gaps left in the scheme of the fundamental correlation can be filled by subsidiary work and social activity. Through manual work an interaction between the natural and social environment is created.

Gandhi takes the general requirements of 'school duty' and 'freedom from fees' in his programme.

Mann (1995: 84) gives a list of daily routine activities which are said to be part of *Basic Education*. Upon which is the School Assembly: In the school assembly the pupils should first of all be informed about local, national and international events. Secondly, they should be told about changes and events in the school community and its immediate environment. Thirdly, the school community should be included in the organizational changes of the daily routine.

To form a harmonic relationship between teacher and pupil the concept of *Basic Education* developed concrete requirements which are associated with the role of teacher. The teacher who is built upon the foundations of *Basic Education* is more like an Indian Guru than a teacher of an English-influenced school. To achieve community, cooperation, etc. in the school community it is suggested that teacher and pupil live together in the village community.

7 Independence, since 1947

India achieved political freedom in 1947 and has transformed into a secular democratic republic. The educational system had to make its contribution to the development of habits, attitudes and qualities of character, which would enable its citizens to bear worthily the responsibilities of democratic citizenship and to counteract separatist tendencies.

The concept of *Basic Education* was officially declared a 'national pattern' for the primary levels I and II (ages 6 – 14) in 1947.

In 1947: 85% of the population was illiterate and only one out of ten students completed the 5th standard.

One of the fundamental rights guaranteed by the Constitution is the right of every citizen of the Union to free and compulsory education up to the age of 14.

The 'Unions Conference' in 1948 came to the conclusion that *Basic Education* should become the obligatory model of education in a period less than forty years and should be introduced into primary schools (ages 6 – 11) within ten years.

In 1964–66 the education ministry commissioned a report to examine the education system. Questions of Basic Education were touched and re-interpreted in the sense of a "manpower approach"(Mann 1995: 90). As a result, instead of knowledge through practical education, knowledge and practical education became the didactic foundation. The reform suggestions of the commission subordinated the education system to economic planning. The goals of educations had to be derived from the national development goals which were dominated primary economically.

The Institute of *Basic Education* in New Delhi, founded in 1956 has been closed. The concept remained a 'political declaration' (Mann 1995: 93). As a result, the vertical structure of the colonial education system was adopted. The post-colonial education system was set up completely analogously in a top-to bottom hierarchy. Universities and Colleges determined the the teaching content of the primary and secondary schools.

Not only knowledge was requited but also social training and the "'inculcation of right ideals"' Singh (2011: 155). Important Questions were the place of the different languages, Hindi and English, the role of education in developing democratic citizenship, the improvement of vocation efficiency, the development of personality through education and education for leadership.

The Kothari Commission, 1964-66 made a comprehensive review of the entire educational system. It was the largest report ever written on education and national development. Main considerations of this report were the introduction of work experience an integral part of general education, the stress on moral education and sense of social responsibility, the vocationalisation of secondary education, the setting up of a small numbers of elite universities, the teacher training and education for agriculture and research in agriculture. Five years of primary education should be provided to all children by 1975-76, Seven years by 1985-86. These goals turned out to be very difficult to reach, because there was an 'explosion' in population. The commission suggested a new pattern of 10 + 2 + 3. It has been a great success since its introduction in 1975.

After comprehensive surveys and studies on different aspects of education, Human Resource Development Ministry, Government of India published a report on National Policy on Education in the first week of May 1986.

Main features of National Policy on Education 1986 were the responsibility of education for the development of individuals and for culture assimilation, the opening of Nevodaya (elite) schools for economically deprived but talented children, women education, education of scheduled castes, Tribes and backward classes, adult education, distance education, and rural universities.

The 10 + 2 + 3 structure is now accepted in all parts of the country. It should have been ensured that all children who attain the age of about 11 by 1990 will have five years of schooling. By 1995, all children should be provided free and compulsory education up to 14 years of age. Children with a special talent should be provided opportunities to proceed faster, by making good quality education available to them, irrespective of their capacity to pay for it.

The Reddy Commission revised the education policy of India in 1992. The 10 + 2 + 3 system was further broke in 5 years of primary education and 3 years of primary education and 2 years of high school. The drop-out levels of 60 Percent should be brought to about 40 to 50 percent.

Navodaya Vidyalas (elite schools) should be established in all the districts of each state of the country and the expenses should be borne by the state government. The children graduating from any Navodaya schools should be given higher education in a school or college considered suitable for them. Central Government should establish a special school for higher education of students who have passed out of Navodaya school. A Central Council of Rural Institutes was to be established to look after the needs of every rural area. All India Councils of Technical Education should be appointed by the central and state governments in order to look after the needs of technical education in their respective areas. This council would set up the minimum standard of facilities which must be made available if such a technical education institution was to be opened.

For the reforms of the examination system, the central and state government had to make a joint effort. Various educational institutions should inform the concerned government of the steps they have taken for reforms of the examination system. The Non-formal education (NFE) has become an accepted alternative channel. The National Council of Educational Research and Training (NCERT) revised school syllabi and brought out revised textbooks for classes I to XII. A Total Literacy Campaign (TLC) was advocated. 35,000 new primary schools, a school system for 180,000,000 children and additional 1,100,000 classrooms were required. The National curricular framework has been carried out. Widening access to secondary education. Professional development of school heads. NCERT has brought out a national curriculum for elementary and secondary education. The Navodaya Vidyalas scheme should cover, all district by 8th five year plan. 50 Navodaya Vidyalas should be opened every year. Admission tests should be evaluated and talented teachers employed. In-service teacher training courses should be envisaged. The students should have facilities for vocational training. Emphasis on national integration and accountability to community. Minimum Levels of Learning (MLL) have been determined, comprehensive continuous evaluation at the elementary stage.

IV Today

India has one of the worst education systems in the world.

As Hemali Chapia writes in the Times of India on June 1st 2013, India backed out of the Programme for International Student Assessment (PISA) in 2009 after participating for the first time. During the examination, 15-year-olds from the two Indian states Tamil Nadu and Himachal Pradesh were put through the PISA evaluation in reading, maths and science. On the global stage, they stood second last among 73 countries, only beating Kyrgyzstan. In Maths the states finished second and third last, beating only Kyrgyzstan; the English test showed the same result and science results were the worst. While Himachal stood last, Tamil Nadu was slightly better and finished third from bottom. Experts estimate that an Indian class VIII student is at the same level as a South Korean class III student in math abilities or a class II student from Shanghai when it comes to English reading skills.

The Indian School system follows the British structure: Primary school consists of grades

I-V (ages 6-11), middle school consists of Standard VI - VIII (ages 11-14).

1 The Ministry of Human Resource and Development

Decisions by the Central Government of India, seated in Delhi are executed by the Ministries. The Ministry responsible for all matters concerning schools and education is the Ministry of Human Resource Development (MHRD). It was created on September 26, 1985. Before that it was called Ministry of Education.

Currently, the MHRD works through two departments:

1. The Department of Higher Education, and

2. The Department of School Education and Literacy

Since the main topic of this thesis is Teaching English as a Foreign Language (TEFL) we are more interested in school education. So we are going to concentrate on second on the Department of School Education and Literacy.

2 The Department of School Education and Literacy

According to Hill and Chalaux (2011), the Department of School Education and Literacy coordinates planning with the states. It consists of nine institutions. Six [6] are rather small and powerless. They are also quite irrelevant for this topic. So we are left with three institutions in one Department of the Ministry of Human Resource Development (MHRD) that might be relevant for the topic.

1. The National Council for Teacher Education (NCTE)

2. The National Council for Educational Research and Training (NCERT)

3. The Central Board of Secondary Education (CBSE)

3 The National Council for Teacher Education

The National Council for Teacher Education (NCTE) is responsible for planning and developing teacher education. It also developed a '"Teacher Eligibility Test (TET)"' to

---

[6] The Central Institute of Education Technology (CIET), the Central Tibetan School Administration (CTSA), the Kendriya Vidyalaya Sangathan (KVS), which is responsible for military and diplomatic schools, the National Bal Bhawan, responsible for extracurricular activities of students students in all ages, the Navodaya Vidyalaya Samiti (NVS), which is concerned with the selection of talented rural children to provide them with high quality education in a residential school system.

select teachers. Such a test is mandatory for getting teaching jobs in government schools from Class 1 to Class 8. But most states conduct their own TET.

The NCTE is responsible for recognizing teacher training institutions. It also edits the "'National Curriculum Framework for Teacher Education"'. The current version is from 2009.

Teacher education in India is different from teacher education in Germany. In India, the teacher education is located at private colleges, but there is a governmental refund (cf. for Education (2009))

The NCERT provides school books online[7]. There even is a mobile-phone application called "'Ncert Books"'. Students and teachers, as well as everybody who is interested can choose a text book from every class form I to XII in form of pdf for every possible subject. According to Hill and Chalaux (2011), the NCERT's textbooks serve as models for the states' syllabuses.

4   The Indian School System

Childhood ends –at the latest– in 8th Standard.

Public exams at the end of grade X and XII drive instruction during the whole secondary level.

Secondary schools are affiliated with central or state boards which administer examinations at the end of 10th standard resulting in the award of the Secondary School Certificate (SSC), the All-India Secondary School Certificate (AISSC) or the Indian Certificate of Secondary Education (ICSE). There are three national examining boards: the Central Board of Secondary Education (CBSE), the Council for the Indian School Certificate Examinations (CISCE) and the National Open School (NOS) for distance education The ICSE, which is conducted by the CISCE and the AISSC, conducted by the CBSE are broadly equivalent, but the AISSC is more popular. The English question bank is "less Shakespearian and more contemporary" (Cheney et al. 2005: 7).

The British Council (in Cheney et al. (2005)) notes that the Indian Secondary School Certificate may generally be considered slightly below the British General Certificate of Secondary Education (GCSE), or the International GCSE High School Examinations Standard. The Content is considered equivalent, but students are not expected to prob-

---

[7]   http://www.ncert.nic.in/ncerts/textbook/textbook.htm; Tuesday 24th March, 2015

lem solve or apply their knowledge in the same way.

5   General Education

The Government drafts five-year plans that include education policy and funding for education. State-level ministries coordinate education programs at the local levels. Urban government schools are overseen by the state education ministry and the municipal government. In rural areas, either the district board or the village council (Panchayat) has oversight on school functioning and appoints teachers.

The states provide the majority of educational funding

There is a national curriculum outline (Table 1) but in reality no-one really cares for it. English is taught much earlier.

6   Higher Secondary Education

The majority of students exit school after Grade X (age: 15). For those who stay, schooling becomes differentiated. Based on their performance on the 10th grade exams, students enter an upper-secondary stream for their last two years of schooling before university: The most prestigious stream is the science stream, the second is commerce, and the third is humanities. There is also a fourth, vocational stream. But it's getting less and less popular. The upper secondary education (XI – XII) is conducted in schools or separate junior colleges. After grade XII, students sit for another set of exams. The Higher Secondary Certificate Examinations determine their higher education options. Good colleges have cut-off marks of over 90% overall score. Based on the stream, the students' course of study is nearly determined, because there are entrance tests at the colleges and universities.

The typical school schedule in secondary school is a 9 period day. One period has 40 minutes.

A picture of the Indian education system can be found in the appendix (Fig. 1)

7   English as a Medium in School

Mother tongue is the medium of instruction for most Indian primary students, although students from elite families are typically sent to English medium schools as English is considered a distinction of class Cheney et al. (2005: 5).

English in India is important for higher education, upward social mobility and has played a key role in establishing India as an economic power globally. Since everybody can speak English, possible employers and foreign capital have small transaction costs. They can just go to India and find an infrastructure like in Great Britain and can talk to nearly everyone without a big language barrier. That is a great advantage in global competition. A stable law system with understandable rules and educated workforce for a cheap price attract international financial capital.

Many states start teaching English as second language in 3rd standard.

Bibliography

J. C. Aggarwal. *Development of Education System in India*. Shipra, Delhi, 2004.

Gretchen Rhines Cheney, Betsy Brown Ruzzi, and Karthik Muralidharan. Improving access and quality in the Indian education system. Technical report, National Center on Education and the Economy, November 2005. URL http://www.teindia.nic.in/files/articles/indian_education_sysytem_by_karthik_murlidharan.pdf.

David Crystal. *English as a global language*. Cambridge University Press, 2012.

National Council Teacher for Education. National Curriculum Framework for Teacher Education – Towards Preparing Professional and Humane Teacher. Technical report, National Council for Teacher Education, New Delh, 2009.

Sam Hill and Thomas Chalaux. Improving access and quality in the Indian education system. Technical report, OECD Publishing, 2011. URL http://ideas.repec.org/p/oec/ecoaaa/885-en.html.

Braj B Kachru. The English language in the outer circle. *World Englishes*, pages 241–255, 2006.

N Krishnaswamy and Lalitha Krishnaswamy. *The Story of English in India*. Foundation Books, 2006.

T. B. Macaulay. Minute by the Hon'ble T. B. Macaulay, dated the 2nd February, 1835. URL http://www.columbia.edu/itc/mealac/pritchett/00generallinks/macaulay/txt_minute_education_1835.html.

Bernhard Mann. *The pedagogical and political concepts of Mahatma Gandhi and Paulo Freire : a comparative study on developmental and strategic political education in the Third World*. Hamburg : Krämer, 1995. ISBN 3926952970. Translation of: Die Pädagogisch-politischen Konzeptionen Mahatma Gandhis und Paulo Freires.

Debi Prasanna Pattanayak. *Multilingualism in India*. Multilingual Matters, 1990.

Dr. Yogesh Kumar Singh. *History of Indian Education System*. A. P. H., New Delhi, 2011.

List of Figures

1   Structure of the Indian Education System. Source:Hill and Chalaux (2011)   26

2   Lord Curzon,Source:http://www.britannica.com/EBchecked/topic/147273/
     George-Nathaniel-Curzon-Marquess-Curzon 28

List of Abbreviations

MLL   Minimum Levels of Learning 20

NFE   Non-formal education 19

NCERT National Council of Educational Research and Training 19

TLC   Total Literacy Campaign 19

EIC   East India Company 1

ELTI   English Language Teaching Institute 4

TELI   Teaching English Literature 5

PISA   Programme for International Student Assessment 20

MHRD   Ministry of Human Resource Development 21

TET   Teacher Eligibility Test 21

NCTE   National Council for Teacher Education 21

NCERT National Council of Educational Research and Training 19

SSC   Secondary School Certificate 22

AISSC All-India Secondary School Certificate 22

ICSE   Indian Certificate of Secondary Education 22

CBSE   Central Board of Secondary Education 22

CISCE Council for the Indian School Certificate Examinations 22

GCSE   British General Certificate of Secondary Education 22

RIE   Regional Institute of English for South India 4

Appendix

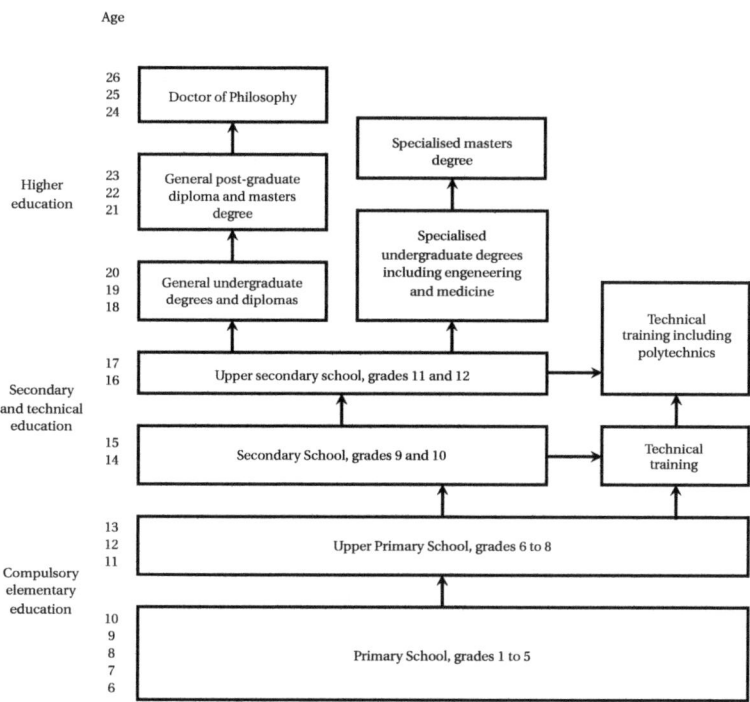

Figure 1: Structure of the Indian Education System. Source:Hill and Chalaux (2011)

Primary School	I and II:	1. One Language: the Mother tongue 2. Mathematics 3. The Art of Healthy and Productive Living
	III to V:	1. One Language: The Mother Tongue 2. Mathematics 3. Environmental Studies 4. The Art of Healthy and Productive Living
Middle School	VI to VIII	1. Three languages: Mother Tongue, Hindi and English 2. Mathematics 3. Science and Technology 4. Social Science 5. Work / Pre-Vocational Education 6. Art Education (fine Arts: Visual and Performing) 7. Heath and Physical Education
Secondary School	IX to X	1. Three languages 2. Mathematics 3. Science and Technology 4. Social Sciences 5. Work Education / Pre-Vocational Education 6. Art Education (fine Arts: Visual and Performing) 7. Heath and Physical Education

Table 1: National Curriculum Outline